VERY SMALL HORSES

LIVING THEIR GREATEST LIVES

VERY SMALL HORSES
LIVING THEIR GREATEST LIVES

Amy Lewis

Smith Street Books

$\mathcal{B}$e
THE WIND
BENEATH
YOUR OWN
MANE.

THEY CAN PUT A SADDLE ON YOUR BACK, BUT THEY CAN'T TELL YOUR TINY LEGS WHERE TO GO.

WHEN THE ROAD DIVERGES INTO TWO PATHS, TAKE A BREAK AND ROLL AROUND IN THE DUST.

YOU CAN BE ANYTHING YOU WANT TO BE. EXCEPT FOR A REGULAR-SIZED HORSE.

YOUR BODY MAY BE SMALL, BUT YOUR HEART IS (LITERALLY) MUCH LARGER THAN MOST MAMMALS.

SOMETIMES YOU MUST GALLOP THROUGH THE TALLEST GRASS TO FIND YOUR STABLEMATES.

THE RAINY DAYS MAKE DELICIOUS GRASS GROW FASTER.

Vulnerability is your strength, as is the ability to crush cans with your hooves.

It COULD BE WORSE — YOU COULD BE A MINIATURE DONKEY.

WHEN SOMEONE WRONGS YOU, WAIT UNTIL THEY ARE DISTRACTED AND GIVE THEM A BITE.

Fear IS THE ROTTEN CARROT IN YOUR TROUGH. TASTE IT, KNOW IT, AND SPIT IT OUT.

IF YOU REACH
A DEAD END,
DON'T BE AFRAID
TO TURN AROUND
WITH YOUR TAIL
HELD HIGH.

GRAZE UPON THE MEADOWS OF YOUR DREAMS AND BUCK OFF YOUR FEARS.

IN A FIELD OF HORSES, BE A UNICORN.

TREAT YOUR MANE WITH LOVE AND CARE — THE BEST REVENGE IS HAVING GREAT HAIR.

*I*F SOMEONE TAKES YOU FOR A RIDE, YOU HAVE THE POWER TO BUCK THEM OFF.

Your legs
may be tiny,
but they
can carry
a great load.

LIFE CAN BE HECTIC — DON'T FORGET TO TAKE A MOMENT TO MUNCH ON THE ROSES.

IN A PARTY
FULL OF SHOW
PONIES, IT'S
OKAY TO BE
THE ONLY ONE
WITH A LONG
FACE.

WHEN YOUR FACE IS SWARMING WITH FLIES, HEAD TO THE NEAREST POND.

Forgive THE PERSON THAT CHANGES YOUR SHOES AND CHIPS OFF THE DIRT FROM YOUR FILTHY HOOVES.

INSPIRATION CAN COME FROM ANYWHERE: A SONG, A FRIEND, OR AN UNATTENDED CARROT CROP.

If YOU ALWAYS POINT YOUR FACE TOWARD THE WIND, YOU'LL NEVER HAVE TO SMELL WHAT YOU JUST ROLLED AROUND IN.

If SOMEONE
TRIES TO RAIN
ON YOUR PARADE,
STOP IN THE
MIDDLE OF
THE ROUTE
AND LIE DOWN.

MAKE
A LIST OF
ALL OF YOUR
WORRIES AND
THEN STAMP
ON IT.

YOU ARE IN CONTROL OF YOUR DESTINY. AND ANYTHING MANURE-SHAPED THAT'S LEFT ALONG THE WAY.

IN A STABLE
FULL OF 10s,
BE THE 6 WITH
THE BIGGEST
SUGAR CUBE.

When you lose your path, don't be afraid to ask for a helping hoof.

EAT ALL THE APPLES LIFE THROWS AT YOU: THE SEEDS WILL GROW INTO SNACKS FOR LATER.

*L*IFE ISN'T ABOUT HOW HIGH YOU CAN JUMP — IT'S ABOUT THE NUMBER OF HURDLES YOU LEAVE IN YOUR WAKE.

Make your own luck, and if you can, make a friend wherever you go.

THE FIRST APPLE YOU TASTE MAY BE DELICIOUS, BUT DON'T BE AFRAID TO TAKE A BITE OF EVERY KIND.

If YOUR
BELLY HANGS
INCHES FROM
THE GROUND,
IT MEANS THAT
THE BEST
ORCHARD HAS
BEEN FOUND.

WHEN YOU FIND YOUR HOOVES STUCK IN THE MUD, LOOK UP AND TAKE IN THE WORLD.

It's never too late to start over (unless you are 100 in horse years).

The world can feel heavy, but at least you're too small to pull a plow.

Demand to be pampered on only two occasions — night and day.

DON'T SAVE ALL YOUR CARROTS FOR A RAINY DAY. WHEN THE WINTER COMES, SO WILL HAY!

*A*NY BAD DAY
CAN BE TURNED
AROUND BY A
NEW PAIR OF
SHINY DESIGNER
STIRRUPS.

THE SHORTER
YOU ARE,
THE BETTER
PEOPLE CAN
ADMIRE YOUR
GIANT NATURAL
LASHES.

You may never win the Kentucky Derby, but you don't have to spend your weekends training.

Watch THE SUNSET AND LET YOUR PROBLEMS FLOAT INTO THE SKY WITH THE DANDELION TUFTS.

THE GRASS
IS ALWAYS
GREENER WHERE
YOU HAVEN'T
BEEN MUNCHING.

THINK OUTSIDE
OF THE BOX,
YOUR STABLE,
AND THE FIELDS
YOU GALLOP IN.

YOUR BODY IS LIMITED, BUT YOUR IMAGINATION IS INFINITE.

Smith Street Books

Published in 2023 by Smith Street Books
Naarm (Melbourne) | Australia
smithstreetbooks.com

ISBN: 978-1-9227-5460-8

Smith Street Books respectfully acknowledges the Wurundjeri People of the Kulin Nation, who are the Traditional Owners of the land on which we work, and we pay our respects to their Elders past and present.

Publisher: Paul McNally
Editor: Avery Hayes
Text: Amy Lewis
Design and layout: Stephanie Spartels

Printed & bound in China by C&C Offset Printing Co., Ltd.

Book 288
10 9 8 7 6 5 4 3 2 1

MIX
Paper | Supporting
responsible forestry
FSC® C008047
FSC
www.fsc.org

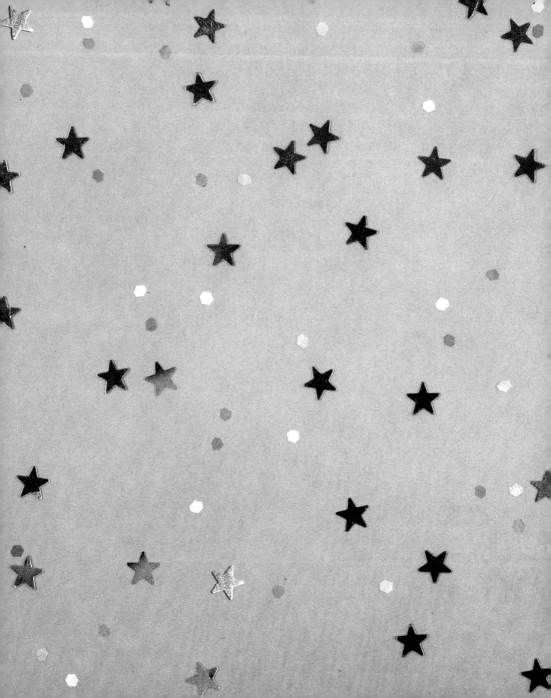